Discover Butterflies & Moths

by Victoria Marcos

© 2014 by Victoria Marcos
ISBN: 978-1-62395-464-2
eISBN: 978-1-62395-465-9
ePib ISBN: 978-1-62395-700-1
Images licensed from Fotolia.com
All rights reserved.
No portion of this book may be reproduced without express permission of the publisher.
First Edition
Published in the United States by Xist Publishing
www.xistpublishing.com
PO Box 61593 Irvine, CA 92602

Butterflies and moths are part of the same order of insects, Lepidoptera.

Butterflies have brightly colored wings and flutter when they fly.

Surprisingly, moths can be as colorful as butterflies.

You may not see many of them since most moths are nocturnal.

3

Butterflies have thin antennae with small balls or clubs at the ends.

Moth antennae have various appearances like this one that looks like two fans.

5

There are approximately 15,000-20,000 species of butterflies and 160,000 of species of moths. New species are still being discovered.

There are more than 750 species of butterflies and 11,000 species of moths that have been discovered in the United States and Canada. They are found on every continent except Antarctica.

Butterflies and moths have four different life stages.

1st STAGE
ovum or egg

2nd STAGE
larva or caterpillar

3rd STAGE
pupa or chrysalis

4th STAGE
imago or adult

Some butterflies and moths species lay their eggs on either on the top or the bottom side of leaves.

Some species lay their eggs on trunks or branches of trees. Most eggs, or ovum, hatch within a few weeks.

Caterpillars, or larva, eat leaves and spend most of their time searching for food. As caterpillars mature they begin to develop wings under their skin.

When caterpillars are fully grown, they look for a plant, tree, leaf or even go underground where they can go onto the next stage of life.

Now, the caterpillar will build a chrysalis as a protective cover during metamorphosis.

During this time, they can't move are are mostly defenseless.

Some species can make sounds or vibrations to scare off predators. Other species have the ability to excrete a toxic chemical as a defense.

15

16

Inside the chrysalis, the pupa begins to form large wings that it will use to fly.

It can take weeks, months or even years for the butterfly or moth to emerge, depending on the species and the weather.

Depending on the species, adult butterflies and moths live from one week to almost a year.

Before it can fly, the newly emerged adult butterfly needs to allow its wings to dry.

During this time it is very vulnerable to predators.

Butterflies feed mostly on nectar from flowers.

They don't carry as much pollen as bees. However, they are capable of carrying the pollen further distances.

Many, but not all, butterflies migrate.

To avoid the cold winter months, every fall Monarchs migrate south to Southern California and mountains in Mexico - places they've never been before.

They will travel up to 2,500 miles to find warm weather.

To avoid being eaten, some moths have evolved to look like less tasty insects, such as wasps, tarantulas and praying mantids.

Some moths even mimic bird droppings. This moth looks like a leaf.

Moth-pollinated flowers are often very fragrant. These plants allow nocturnal moths to easily find flowers after dark.

Although moths don't have noses they have an excellent sense of smell. They use their antennae to identify smells.

While some moths suck nectar, others don't eat at all.

The adult Luna moth doesn't have a mouth.

After it emerges from its chrysalis, it lives for about a week giving it only enough time to mate and lay eggs.

Moths are a big source of food for bats.

Some moths have developed defenses against bats.

Tiger moths make ultrasonic clicking sounds that jam bat sonar, keeping the bat from finding them.

32

Both butterfly and moth caterpillars are one of the most important animals in the ecosystem.

They make abundant food for countless animals.

Plus, butterflies and moths make up a fun and beautiful part of our world!

www.ingramcontent.com/pod-product-compliance
Lightning Source LLC
LaVergne TN
LVHW021600070426
835507LV00014B/1887